STILL PASSING THE POINT

by

Bernard McCall

INTRODUCTION

The first edition of *Passing the Point* was published in June 2005. I have often been asked to produce an updated edition and I am delighted to present this to readers now. Much has happened in the intervening five years. The most obvious change is a reduction in the variety of cargoes handled in our local ports. The closure of the Britannia Zinc smelter at Avonmouth meant the ending of imports of lead and zinc concentrates along with exports of finished products, and the closure of the Sevalco factory brought about the cessation of carbon black feedstock imports. This five-year period has also seen the virtual cessation of refrigerated products being imported by conventional ships and this trade has now been switched almost exclusively to containers although the year prior to publication has seen a reduction of these, too.

One consequence of the changes has been a reduction in the variety of ships illustrated in the pages that follow. We cannot begin with cruise liners because no such vessels have visited the port since the publication of our original volume. It must also be remembered that the world has suffered a huge economic crisis towards the end of this five-year spell between books and seems to be slowly emerging from the crisis as these notes are being written in early 2010. The economic downturn has obviously affected international trade and shipping but our local ports have fared better than some in other areas of the UK.

The vast majority of photographs were taken since the publication of *Passing the Point* but some earlier ones have been included for nostalgia and/or comparisons. I have tried to include once again a representative sample of ships. Some of these may be seen passing Battery Point almost every day, others may call occasionally whilst some may have paid a solitary visit.

My grateful thanks go to the Bristol Port Company, especially Chris Jones and Paul White, for help in providing information about cargoes carried by the ships. As always I must thank Gil Mayes and Iain McCall for reading and correcting initial drafts of the book.

Bernard McCall   *Portishead, Bristol*   *August, 2010*

ABBREVIATIONS

Readers unfamiliar with maritime publications will need an explanation of abbreviations used in this book. TEU is an abbreviation for Twenty-Foot Equivalent Units, a measure of container capacity based on 20' containers. After the name of each ship is an abbreviation of the ship's flag nation as noted in the table below followed by its gross tonnage (gt) and year of construction.

ANT	Netherlands Antilles	DIS	Danish International Register	LBR	Liberia
ATG	Antigua & Barbuda	DNK	Denmark	MAR	Morocco
BEL	Belgium	ESP	Spain	MHL	Marshall Islands
BHS	Bahamas	FIN	Finland	MLT	Malta
BGR	Bulgaria	GIB	Gibraltar	NIS	Norwegian International Register
BRB	Barbados	GBR	United Kingdom	NLD	Netherlands
CHI	People's Republic of China	IOM	Isle of Man	PAN	Panama
DEU	Germany	ITA	Italy	PHL	Philippines

PMD	Madeira
RUS	Russia
SGP	Singapore
SWE	Sweden
THA	Thailand
TUR	Turkey
VCT	St Vincent and the Grenadines
UKR	Ukraine

Published by Bernard McCall, 400 Nore Road, Portishead, Bristol, BS20 8EZ, England. Website : www.coastalshipping.co.uk. Telephone/fax : 01275 846178. E-mail : bernard@coastalshipping.co.uk. All distribution enquiries should be addressed to the publisher.

Printed by Amadeus Press, Ezra House, West 26 Business Park, Cleckheaton, West Yorkshire, BD19 4TQ. Telephone : 01274 863210; fax : 01274 863211. E-mail : info@amadeuspress.co.uk; website : www.amadeuspress.co.uk

ISBN : 978-1-902953-49-6

Front cover: The **MSC Samantha** (PAN, 30657gt/82) was launched at the Aioi yard of Ishikawajima Harima Heavy Industries on 20 January 1982 and named **S. A Vaal** on 22 May with delivery to the South African Marine Corporation Ltd (Safmarine) coming on 3 June 1982. Changes within the structure of her owning company resulted in her being renamed **Vaal** in 1987 then reverting to **S. A. Vaal** in 1996 and **Safmarine Vaal** in 2000. She left Safmarine in 2002 and was renamed **Pacific Sky** and joined the MSC fleet in 2004. On 10 March 2004, she was renamed **MSC Samantha** at Singapore, her name coming from the daughter of Dallas Sutton, long-serving MSC Traffic Manager in Durban. Inward bound at Battery Point on 22 April 2010, she was not a regular caller and made only two visits to Royal Portbury Dock a little over one year prior to this one.

Back cover: The veteran **Orange Star** (LBR, 9981gt/75) has continued to be a regular caller bringing fruit juice from Santos in Brazil. Daytime arrivals and departures of this ship, now 35 years old, are guaranteed to see many enthusiasts on Battery Point wishing to photograph her. She did appear in *Passing the Point* but, as there are now so few vessels of such conventional design, we make no excuse for using another image of her, albeit a rather distant one. She was built at Smith's Dock on the River Tees as **Andalucia Star** for the Blue Star Line. Renamed **Fife** in 1984 and then **Orange Star** in 1986, she was converted in 1987 from a conventional refrigerated dry cargo ship to a tanker/cargo ship by the fitting of six tankers to carry fruit juice. We see her in wintry conditions on 9 January 2010.

In the absence of cruise liners, we begin with a view of one of the Grimaldi vehicle carriers which call at Royal Portbury Dock up to twice each week. Perhaps not many readers realise that these are also passenger vessels and it is possible to book a short "cruise" on one of them, calling at ports in Ireland, Denmark, Sweden and Belgium, or a month-long round trip to the Mediterranean. The **Grande Mediterraneo** (ITA, 51714gt/98), inward bound from Setubal on 30 March 2008, was built at the Fincantieri shipyard in Castellammare di Stabia on the Gulf of Naples. She is driven by a 2-stroke 7-cylinder Sulzer engine of 21140bhp. She has a capacity of 4650 cars on ten decks, three of which are hoistable to allow high vehicles to be carried. She offers accommodation for twelve passengers in six cabins.

The **Auto Bank** (FIN,19107gt/98) was built as a roll on / roll off cargo vessel at the Umoe Sterkoder shipyard in Kristiansund, Norway, from where she was handed over on 7 August 1998 and officially named *Serenaden* three days later. She entered service between Kemi in Finland and Lübeck in Germany, the Finnish terminal switching to Hamina in November 2004. She thus became a regular sight on the Kiel Canal through northern Germany but it was the Suez Canal that she passed on 7 October 2006 as she was on passage via Sharjah and Dubai to Nantong in China where she was converted from a roll-on / roll-off vessel to a vehicle carrier. The work had been completed by early January 2007 and she sailed to South Korea to load for northern Europe, heading for Rotterdam via Tarragona and Vigo. Taken on long-term time charter by United European Car Carriers (UECC), she was renamed **Auto Bank** but retained the funnel colours of her owners, Bore, part of the Rettig Group in Finland. Her two sisterships have been similarly converted and chartered by UECC. Power comes from a 4-stroke 16-cylinder Wärtsilä engine of 19686bhp. She has a capacity of 1610 cars. We see her at the end of a voyage from Pasajes on 2 March 2008 when she was carrying a cargo of mainly Vauxhall Corsa cars for UK distribution.

A regular visitor to Royal Portbury Dock, the **Autosun** (PMD, 21094gt/00), was photographed on 21 April 2010 at the end of a voyage from Pasajes. She is the last of three similar sister vessels built at the Numakuma shipyard of the Tsuneishi Shipbuilding Co Ltd for UECC. She is powered by two 4-stroke 8-cylinder Wärtsilä engines each of 11421bhp which give her a maximum speed of 20.9 knots. She has a capacity of 1400 cars. She carries the new UECC livery which was applied in drydock at Falmouth during a period of extended overhaul in December 2008.

The **Equine** (PAN, 16948gt/79), inward bound from Vlissingen (Flushing) in the Netherlands on 4 September 2007 during a series of five voyages bringing Ford cars to Avonmouth, is another vehicle carrier to have been converted. Built as **Eva Oden** at the Oresundsvarvet yard in Landskrona, Sweden, she was launched on 18 May 1979 and completed on 14 September 1979. She entered service between the ports of Gothenburg, Ghent, Felixstowe and Immingham. On 6 December 1987, she arrived at Flensburg to undergo considerable modification at the Flensburger shipyard. An additional cargo section was added which increased her length by 17 metres. She was also fitted with new propulsion machinery, her original two 4-stroke 16-cylinder Alpha diesels each of 7680bhp being replaced by two 4-stroke 6-cylinder Wärtsilä Vee engines each of 6118bhp. She was chartered by DFDS Tor Line for ten years and was renamed **Tor Belgia**, reverting to **Eva Oden** on 29 November 1998 upon the cessation of this charter. She had continued to work on her original route since entering service but in 1999 was trading between southern Norway and Europoort. On 16 May 2000 she left Zeebrugge and entered service between that port and Immingham or London. She became **Equine** on 22 October 2006. She had three passenger cabins offering twelve berths for drivers. In early 2010 she was renamed **Winner 6** but only briefly as she arrived at Alang for demolition on 14 February 2010, being beached six days later.

There are several examples in this book that illustrate the complex question of ship ownership, management and operation. The **Maersk Wind** (SGP, 51770gt/00), inward bound from Nagoya with 1605 Toyota cars on 2 May 2005, is our first example. She was built by the Hashihama Shipbuilding Co Ltd at Tadotsu in Japan for A P Møller. Power comes from a 2-stroke 8-cylinder Mitsubishi engine of 19,200bhp. She has a capacity of 5240 cars housed on 13 decks of which 3 are hoistable. The Møller - Maersk car carriers were time chartered to two operators, one of which was Wallenius Lines, founded by Olof Wallenius, whose funnel colours the ship wears in this photograph. At the end of 2007, Møller/Maersk decided to sell its entire fleet of car carriers to Höegh Autoliners and this company owns the **Maersk Wind** but the time charter to Wallenius continues.

The **World Island** (PAN, 41035gt/84) was built by Sumitomo Heavy Industries Ltd at its Oppama shipyard in Yokosuka where she was launched on 28 January 1984, delivery to her owners being made in June of that year. Her builder supplied the 2-stroke 8-cylinder Sulzer engine of 15360bhp. For the first ten years of her career, she was named **World Wing II.** She had a capacity of just over 5000 cars. The decline in vehicle sales during the world recession saw many vehicle carriers laid up or sold for demolition. Now 25 years old, demolition was inevitable and she arrived for recycling at Xinhui in July 2009. In this photograph with the tug **Portgarth** alongside, she is inward bound from Quang Zhou on 11 February 2008 and carrying 1322 Honda cars. She made a total of 24 voyages to Royal Portbury Dock during her life.

With an overall length of just under 265 metres, the **Taronga** (NIS, 54826gt/96) is one of the longest ships to appear in this book. She was built by Mitsubishi Heavy Industries Ltd at Nagasaki and she is powered by a 2-stroke 7-cylinder engine of 30439 bhp manufactured by the shipbuilder. We see her outward bound on 22 July 2000 after discharging a cargo of forest products from the USA. In January 2003, she went to the Nantong shipyard on the estuary of the Yangtse River in China where she was converted to a dedicated vehicles carrier. She now has nine decks and *Lloyd's Register* notes that she is able to carry 4923 cars compared to the 573 at the time of the photograph. She had a 2833TEU container capacity but this has now disappeared in favour of additional vehicle decks. She is no longer seen in the Bristol Channel but is a frequent visitor to Southampton.

Having seen some vehicle carriers after conversion from roll on / roll off ferries, we now go back in time a few years to see such a ferry prior to conversion. The date was 14 February 1988 and the **Mercandian Prince II** (DNK, 7955grt/84) was approaching Avonmouth at the end of a voyage from the Bulgarian port of Bourgas via Limassol. Her cargo was mainly trailers carrying fruit and vegetables. The ship was built in Denmark by Frederikshavn Værft & Tørdok and was one of 79 ships built at this yard between 1966 and 1987 for Per Henriksen's Mercandia shipping company. She was the seventh in a series of nine similar ferries built at the yard for Mercandia. She was launched on 7 October 1983 and delivered on 3 February the following year. Renamed **Ferrymar I** on 10 November 1988 for the duration of a charter to Compagnie Marocaine de Navigation (COMANAV), she reverted to her original name on 23 May 1991. Sold to Greek owners on 1 December 1994, she was renamed **Neptune Olympic** and was converted to a vehicle carrier in 1995.

The first of three very similar ships built for Scanscot Shipping Services, the **Scan Atlantic** (IOM, 8821gt/99) is a product of the Peenewerft shipyard in Wolgast. She is certainly a multipurpose vessel. Her stern ramp allows her to carry roll on / roll off cargoes and she has a 628TEU container capacity. She has two holds but a single hatch served by two 150-tonne cranes so she can also carry heavy lift project cargoes. She is fitted with two decks, one of which is hoistable. Power comes from a 4-stroke 12-cylinder B&W engine of 7831bhp. We see her outward bound to Kuwait with a cargo of 156 accommodation units on 22 August 2008.

The **Alida Gorthon** (SWE, 12750gt/77) is an unusual vessel. She was built as a bulk carrier by the Korea Shipbuilding & Engineering Corp in Busan, being launched on 27 October 1976 and delivered in January 1977. On 7 September 1990 she arrived at Hamburg and was there converted to a cargo ship equipped for the carriage of palletised cargo. She left the German port on 22 December. Clearly visible on her starboard side in this view are the two side ramps which are used by fork lift trucks to load pallets of newsprint rolls. Also visible is the single crane, although *Lloyd's Register* continues to note that she has two 30-tonne cranes, this referring to the travelling gantry cranes she carried when trading as a bulk carrier. We see her passing Battery Point on 13 March 1999 at the end of a voyage with a cargo of newsprint from Corner Brook in Canada.

The **Zui Yoh** (PHL, 38844gt/90) is a good example of a specialised design of bulk carrier. She was built as a woodchip carrier with six holds and six hatches served by three 14,7 tonne cranes. A distinctive feature above deck level are the hoppers into which the woodchips are tipped during loading. These vessels were all built in the Far East and are a feature of maritime trade in that part of the world. The **Zui Yoh** was built at the Mizushima yard of the Sanoyas Corporation. She was launched on 20 November 1989 and delivered in March the following year. She is powered by a 2-stroke 6-cylinder Mitsubishi engine of 7945bhp. She arrived at Royal Portbury Dock on 6 May 2006 with a cargo of 41,500 tonnes of soya from San Lorenzo on the River Paraná in Argentina.

Chipolbrok is the abbreviated title of the Chinese-Polish Joint Stock Shipping Company which was established on 15 June 1951 and was the first ever Sino-foreign deed of association following the proclamation of the People's Republic of China. Initially each country provided six ships to the company and the aim was to transport goods necessary for the mutual development of the two communist countries. The company has overcome many economic and political problems to remain active in its original role and also to provide liner services on a wider basis.

It has seen a continuing need for multipurpose vessels, the **Jia Xing** (CHI, 18177gt/92) being an example. She has a 1054 TEU container capacity and also has four 24.5 tonne cranes to handle general cargo. She was built by "3 Maj" Brodogradiliste shipyard in Rijeka and was launched as **Bao Zheng** but entered service as **Jia Xing**. She is seen on 25 April 2007 almost at the end of a voyage from China to Royal Portbury Dock with a cargo of forest products.

Because the Chipolbrok fleet has always comprised multipurpose vessels, it has tended to retain older ships longer than many other operators. The **Carnival** (MLT, 18772gt/77) is a good example. She was built by Nippon Kokan KK at Tsu in Japan as **Tysla** for Wilh Wilhelmsen whose vehicle carriers are a frequent sight passing Battery Point. She was launched on 7 June 1977 and handed over to her Norwegian owner on 20 September. Her name was modified to **Willine Tysla** when transferred to an associated company in 1982. Four years later, she was acquired by Chipolbrok and renamed **Cai Lun**, becoming **Carnival** in 1991. She arrived in Royal Portbury Dock with over 5,600 tonnes of plywood on 19 June 2005 after a voyage from Singapore via Aqaba and we see her as she sailed to Rotterdam on the evening of 22 June. She was sold to other Chinese operators in summer 2008 and was renamed **Golden Bridge** on 7 July.

Ships operated by the Sanko Line in Japan have always had hulls painted in a distinctive light green colour. They have often retained this colour after being sold out of the fleet. The *Fuat Bey* (TUR, 16582gt/85) was built as *Sanko Splendour* by Mitsubishi Heavy Industries Ltd in Nagasaki. She was launched on 13 April 1985 and delivered during July. She is powered by a 2-stroke 6-cylinder Mitsubishi engine of 6570bhp. She was acquired by her Turkish owners and renamed *Fuat Bey* in 1997, being handed over at Yokosuka on 25 November. On 26 November 2009, we see her approaching Avonmouth from Antwerp to load 20,500 tonnes of scrap for the Turkish port of Iskenderun.

The **Angelina F** (PAN, 19340gt/84) has much in common with the **Fuat Bey**. She, too, was originally in the Sanko Line fleet but she has lost her green hull in favour of black. Originally named **Sanko Heart**, she was built by Mitsubishi Heavy Industries Ltd but at the company's yard in Shimonoseki and with her four 25-tonne cranes she typifies the geared bulk carriers built in the Far East in the mid-1980s with the timber trade in mind. She is fitted with an identical engine to that of the **Fuat Bey**. She was launched on 10 July 1984 and delivered four months later.

After a decade as **Sanko Heart** she was sold and renamed **Aurora Opal** in early October 1994. A further decade elapsed and she became **Angelina F** on 3 June 2004. This name was to prove rather short lived as she was renamed **SJN Orcas** on 5 June 2005 and then **Sifnos Pride** on 12 March 2007. The low afternoon sun on 21 December 2004 highlights the second Severn road bridge and, beyond that, the Wye bridge as she passes Battery Point at the start of a voyage carrying scrap metal to Karachi.

Another arrival to load scrap was the **Mallika Naree** (THA, 13880gt/84) a further typical product of the Japanese shipyards in the mid-1980s. She was built by K. K. Uwajima Zosensho at Uwajima for Japanese owners and was originally named **Koryu Maru**. She was launched on 9 February 1984 and delivered to her owners in April of that year. Her first change of name came in 1989 when she was renamed **Puff**, later becoming **Ocean Aya** in 1990, and **Keyera** then **Mallika Naree** in 1995 when acquired by Precious Shipping Ltd, one of the leading shipowning companies in Thailand. On 9 May 1999, she had the distinction of being the first vessel to load 'Boodarie Iron' briquettes from a new but remarkably short-lived iron ore processing plant in Western Australia. She has four holds and four hatches served by three 25-tonne cranes. She is powered by a 2-stroke 6-cylinder Mitsubishi engine of 6000bhp. The photograph was taken on 23 September 2008 as she arrived from Morocco to load for India. In February 2009 she was sold to Chinese owners and renamed **Wu Feng** under the Panamanian flag.

We now look at four ships representing standard designs from former communist countries. During the 1970s and 1980s, the Georgi Dimitrov shipyard in the Bulgarian port of Varna built a huge number of bulk carriers for the country's own state-controlled merchant fleet and for countries such as Cuba, Poland and Romania that were, along with Russia, members of what was known as the Comecon bloc. The **Milin Kamak** (BGR, 16166gt/79) is one of a class of over sixty bulk carriers built at the yard between 1973 and 1984. About a quarter of them were built for the Bulgarian fleet and the vast majority of the others were destined for Comecon fleets. Over twenty examples were delivered to Russia. She is driven by a 2-stroke 6-cylinder Sulzer engine of 12000bhp. We see her arriving from Gibraltar on 20 May 2009. She loaded a cargo of 20,000 tonnes of wheat in Royal Portbury Dock and departed for Tarragona three days later. Milin Kamak is a hill in north-west Bulgaria.

The **Liliana Dimitrova** (BGR, 23779gt/82) is an example of a larger bulk carrier design from the Georgi Dimitrov shipyard. The first six examples were built for Poland and this ship was the fourth of five built for Bulgaria; a further eleven were delivered to owners in other countries. She is one of the later examples to be built and is fitted with four 25 tonne cranes. Her 2-stroke 8-cylinder B&W engine gives 15000bhp. She was photographed on 6 July 2003 as she neared the end of a voyage from Santos in Brazil with a cargo of 14,370 tonnes of animal feed. Although piracy off the Horn of Africa has hit the headlines only comparatively recently, this vessel was attacked by pirates on 3 May 1995. She was not captured but one crew member was injured by gunfire during the attack which happened about 100 miles west of the remote Yemeni island of Suqutra. The ship is named after a famous Bulgarian gymnast who went on to coach part of the Canadian gymnastics team.

The import of coal continues to be a vital trade for the Bristol Port Company. As will be seen shortly, these imports are brought by large and rather characterless bulk carriers but a few years ago vessels from the fleet of the Polish Steamship Company were regular callers. Inward bound on 13 October 2005 is the **Powstaniec Styczniowy** (MLT, 21531gt/86) with 33,540 tonnes of coal from Riga. She was the sixth of seven sisterships delivered to her Polish owners by Stocznia Szczecinska and designated as Type B542. They were followed by five Type B545 vessels for a different Polish company and two further examples for the state-controlled merchant fleet of Czechoslovakia. She has five hatches serving five holds and is driven by a 2-stroke 6-cylinder Sulzer engine of 13230bhp. The **Powstaniec Styczniowy** was launched on 18 October 1985 and delivered on 18 July 1986. Her name, meaning "January Insurgent", refers to a participant in the uprising which started on 22 January 1863 when young Polish men objected to conscription into the Russian army.

Two months later the **Uniwersytet Slaski** (MLT, 20357gt/79) was noted outward bound to Hull on 10 December 2005 after discharging coal also from Riga. Also built at Stocznia Szczecinska, she is an example of an earlier standard design, namely Type B517. This design followed directly from Type B447 which was built between 1970 and 1975. Both types had nine hatches serving seven holds but for the observer the main distinguishing feature of the B517 vessels was the twin funnels which helped to give them a rather stylish appearance. She has a 2-stroke 6-cylinder Sulzer engine of 12000 bhp. She was launched on 22 December 1978 and delivered on 30 May 1979. Her name refers to the University of Silesia in the Polish city of Wroclaw.

The vast majority of large bulk carriers calling at Royal Portbury Dock do not have any cargo handling gear. With four 30-tonne cranes, the **Nordpol** (DIS, 40066gt/02) was a comparatively rare exception. She was also unusual in being owned in northern Europe, her owners being Danish. She was built by Kanasashi Heavy Industries Co Ltd at Toyohashi, again in Japan, and completed in May 2002. Power comes from a 2-stroke 7-cylinder B&W engine of 15015bhp. When photographed on 27 January 2008, she was outward bound to the Russian port of Ust Luga after discharging 64,890 tons of coal from Murmansk.

Imports of coal arrive mainly from Australia, Colombia, South Africa, Russia and Latvia. Occasionally it is a transhipped cargo which is delivered and on 19 June 2008 the *Catriena* (MLT, 38364gt/98) brought 72,357 tonnes of coal from Rotterdam. We see her departing three days later. The bulk carrier was built for Japanese owners at the Yokosuka shipyard of Sumitomo Heavy Industries Ltd. She was delivered as *Century Fortune* in July 1998. In late 2006, she was acquired by German interests and at the end of December was renamed *Catriena*. Power comes from a 2-stroke 7-cylinder Sulzer engine of 12070bhp. Clearly visible to the right of the photograph is Portishead's open air swimming pool, opened in April 1962. Originally hot water was delivered to the pool up to five times daily by road tanker from the Albright & Wilson chemical works adjacent to Portishead dock. An oil-fired boiler was installed on the site in 1969.

Spot the difference - apart from the ship. The fact that the previous caption discussed the open-air swimming pool is a huge clue. Having been taken over from the local council by trustees, the pool was the subject of a huge refurbishment project undertaken by a team led by American television star Ty Pennington, known for his popular show "Extreme Makeover Home Edition". During one week in mid-May 2009, as part of the programme "Ty's Great British Adventure" shown on a satellite television channel, work estimated to have cost over £200,000 saw the pool transformed. Inward bound on 1 June 2009 with 59,731 tonnes of coal from Ust Luga is the *Pierre* (MLT, 36559gt/96). She too came from a Japanese shipyard, this being the Mizushima yard of Sanoyas Hishino Meisho. She was delivered in February 1996 as *Rialto* and became *Pierre* in summer 2007.

The **Navios Sagittarius** (PAN, 38849gt/06) was built by Sanoyas Hishino Meisho Corp at Kurashiki in Japan and was delivered in November 2006. She is powered by a 2-stroke 7-cylinder B&W engine of 12,200bhp. She was outward bound to Hamburg on 30 March 2008 after discharging a part cargo of 22,047 tonnes of coal from Santa Marta in Colombia. From delivery by her builders, the ship was chartered for two years to BHP Billiton, one of the world's leading mining companies, at a rate of $26,750 per day. Once this had expired, German chemical company Daiichi took her on charter for a further two years but by this time the rate had risen to a daily rate of $64,000. These figures give some idea of the costs involved in owning, operating and chartering large ships.

Another bulk carrier leaving Royal Portbury Dock after discharging a part cargo of coal was the **Ruby Indah** (SGP, 43217gt/98). She had discharged only 10,009 tonnes of Colombian coal and on 7 June 2008 was heading for the Mississippihaven in Rotterdam to discharge the remainder of her cargo. Her draught on departure was still over eleven metres and it was deemed advisable for her to have a tug escort. One tug followed her to the English & Welsh Grounds whilst three others had assisted her out of the dock but had left her by the time she reached the Welsh Hook buoy. The ship was built by the Mitsui Engineering & Shipbuilding Co Ltd at Tamano in Japan. She is powered by a 2-stroke 5-cylinder B&W engine of 13900bhp.

In 1730, brothers Ralph and Robert Clarke, of North Shields, began to buy shares in sailing ships. Robert had two sons, John and Ralph, the former of whom married Jane Stephenson in 1775 and they moved to London where they set up business as ship owners. Their offspring maintained the business and in 1850 Stephenson Clarke & Company was formed and this would become one of the leading companies in British shipowning, becoming part of the Powell Duffryn Group in 1928. The company's ships were characterised by the silver band on the funnel and the naming scheme after towns and villages in Sussex. The **Donnington** (IOM, 7788gt/75) was the first of a pair of ships that were the biggest in the fleet and were built at the Verolme shipyard in Heusden. She was launched on 3 May 1975 and delivered in August. We see her passing Battery Point with 11,725 tonnes of coal from Russia on 11 July 2007 when she was almost at the end of her career in northern Europe. Within a month, she had been taken over by Italian owners and renamed **Sider Genova**.

In 1970, William Robertson Shipowners Ltd also became part of the Powell Duffryn Group. Its ships had always been named after precious and semi-precious gems and consequently the company was also known as Gem Line. In November 1992 two second-hand ships were bought from Spanish owners by Stephenson Clarke Ltd and were given traditional Robertson names. The **Gem** (GBR, 7482gt/74) was the seventh vessel to carry this name. She was launched at Gijon on 8 February 1974 as **Guardo** and came into Stephenson Clarke ownership in November 1992. Although sold to Norwegian owners in September 1996, she was not renamed **Arendal Bay** until early March 1998. A sale to owners in the United Arab Emirates in July 2000 saw her renamed **Khuula** but this proved to be shortlived as she arrived at Chittagong for demolition on 19 December 2000. We see her on a sunny 11 April 1997 as she arrives with coal from Murmansk. Whilst much of the coal is imported for consumption by power stations, this cargo was delivered to Avonmouth for coal merchant E H Bennett based locally in Shirehampton.

We now look at a selection of container vessels. The South African Marine Corporation Ltd (Safmarine) was established in 1946 but by 1999 ownership was in Greek hands although the Safmarine name has lived on. Two Polish shipyards combined to build the **Safmarine Memling** (MHL, 23732gt/99). Her hull was built by Stocznia Gdanska and she was completed by nearby Stocznia Gdynia. Power comes from a 2-stroke 6-cylinder MAN-B&W engine of 23384bhp. She has a 1835TEU container capacity. She was launched as **Poseidon** on 30 April 1999 but was soon taken on charter and renamed **SCL Memling** immediately before leaving Gdynia on 15 August 1999. Her name was changed to **Safmarine Memling** at Cape Town on 11 August 2002 when she was taken on charter by Safmarine. She was almost at the end of a voyage from Cape Town when photographed on 5 March 2007. This was one of the final arrivals on this service from South Africa.

Following the publication of *Passing the Point*, the Mediterranean Shipping Company (MSC) once again reorganised its feeder services and Royal Portbury Dock has been served on a triangular route linking the Bristol Channel to Antwerp and Dunkerque. The **MSC Katherine Ann** (PAN, 17700gt/85) was a regular caller on the route from 28 May 2004. She was built at the Stocznia Szczecinska shipyard in Poland and exemplifies that yard's B181/430 standard design of which MSC bought three in 2003. These were built as general purpose cargo ships and all were fitted with tall masts and heavy-lift derricks. The other two MSC examples, **MSC Cristiana** and **MSC Leanne**, retained this gear for a while although it was very difficult for gantry cranes to handle containers between the derricks. The **MSC Katherine Ann** had all gear removed prior to entering MSC feeder work. Launched on 7 January 1984 as **Eurosun**, she was delivered in mid-October 1985 as **Aquitania**. It is unclear if she traded as such because before the end of the year she had been renamed **Lanka Amitha** by Sri Lankan charterers. Her later names were **Dr Juan B Alberdi** (1987), **Alter Ego** (1998), **Kota Mutara** (2000), **Alter Ego** (2001) and **MSC Katherine Ann** (2003). She was photographed on 8 October 2008. She arrived off Alang on 19 June 2009 and was beached for demolition five days later.

This vessel was one of the most remarkable survivors in the MSC fleet. Seen on 24 April 2007, the **MSC Mee May** (PAN, 16670gt/70), was built as a general cargo ship at the Hamburg yard of Howaldtswerke-Deutsche Werft (HDW). She was launched on 19 March 1970 and delivered to Hapag-Lloyd as **Erlangen** in July of that year. As built, she had two Stülcken heavy-lift derricks. In 1979 she went to the Bremer Vulkan shipyard in Bremen to be rebuilt as a container ship and she re-entered service as **Erlangen Express**. As part of the rebuilding, she was lengthened by 16,7 metres and widened by 3,3 metres. She was briefly renamed **Incotrans Progress** for a charter in 1981/82 and then reverted to **Erlangen Express** until 1986 when she was renamed **Mee May**. She became **MSC Mee May** in 1994 and had three sisterships in the MSC fleet. She arrived for demolition at Gadani Beach on 8 April 2009.

Surprisingly many ship enthusiasts feel that the modern maritime scene holds little of interest. This can hardly be true when looking at the fleet of container ships operated by the Mediterranean Shipping Company, many of which have a fascinating history. Indeed the company has been very successful in using older vessels in the final stages of their career. Built at the Schlichting-Werft shipyard in Travemünde, the *MSC Jilhan* (PAN, 14068gt/86) was launched as *Sandra K* on 21 February 1986 but entered service in May of that year as *JSS Scandinavia*. Like so many vessels in the MSC fleet, she has had a series of names, becoming *Sea Merchant*, *Sandra K* and *CGM Roussillon* all in 1988 then *Red Sea Europa* (1990), *Contship Italy* (1991), *Kapitan Kurov* (1993) and *MSC Jilhan* in 2004. We see her passing Battery Point on 27 June 2009.

Not all of the ships in the huge MSC fleet are owned, many being on charter. Owned ships have a female name after the MSC prefix, chartered vessels have geographical and other names. The **MSC Rhone** (PAN, 36133gt/79) was built by Mitsubishi Heavy Industries Ltd in Kobe as **Hakuba Maru** for Nippon Yusen Kaisha, a Japanese company whose vehicle carriers frequently pass Battery Point. She was renamed **Arcadian** at Singapore on 27 May 2003 for the duration of a charter in the US Gulf and Caribbean and entered the MSC chartered fleet as **MSC Rhone** on 12 July 2004. We see her on 2 August 2009. In early 2010 she was sold to shipbreakers in India and was beached at Alang on 15 June four days after arrival. The importance of the crew of a rescue boat keeping a close eye on sailors can be seen as the boat attends to the crew of a capsized dinghy.

We move on to container feeder ships. The weekly container service linking Avonmouth to Bilbao via Greenock and Dublin has continued to be successful. Since the demise of Bell Lines which established the route, it has had several operators including Seawheel and it is currently operated by DFDS. The liveries of some of the operators, including Bell Lines, can occasionally be seen on some of the containers being carried. The size of vessel serving the route has steadily increased and on 22 May 2005, the **Endeavor** (NLD, 7642gt/05) passes Battery Point. Her hull was built at Mangalia by Daewoo-Mangalia Heavy Industries and towed to the Netherlands for completion at the Volharding Shipyard in Foxhol. She has a 750 TEU capacity. Of special interest is the wooden nameboard affixed to the front of her bridge, a splendid traditional touch by her Harlingen-based owners JR Shipping.

One of the most successful European shipbuilding yards has been that of J J Sietas at Neuenfelde on the outskirts of Hamburg. From the mid-1950s onwards, the yard saw the benefits of series building and the yard's naval architects have been quick to assess developing trends in sea transport and designing ships ready to meet these trends. All have the standard designs with an identifying label and the **Petuja** (DEU, 6362gt/97) is an example of the Type 160 container feeder design with a 700TEU container capacity. She was launched as **Petuja** but delivered to her German owner on 19 April 1997 as **Joanna Borchard** and as such she entered service on the Borchard Lines service from London, Rotterdam and Antwerp to Limassol, Alexandria and Haifa. On 21 November 2000, she reverted to **Petuja** and traded from northern Europe to the Iberian peninsula. By the end of 2001, she was linking Antwerp to Gdynia, Århus and Copenhagen but soon settled into a service from Hamburg and Bremerhaven to Scandinavia. She arrived in Bilbao from Hamburg, however, on 3 January 2008 and took over the weekly service linking the Spanish port to Avonmouth, Greenock and Dublin. She left Avonmouth on her final round trip on 7 March 2010 and sailed from Bilbao to Rotterdam for drydocking and thence to Emden for lay up. She departed on 8 June for Europoort where she was renamed **WEC Franz Hals** and left for Casablanca two days later.

The *Victoria* (ATG, 3999gt/98) is another product of the J J Sietas shipyard. Smaller than the Type 160 *Petuja*, she is an example of the Type 151 design that was introduced in 1993 and had a 508TEU container capacity. She was launched on 19 January 1998 and delivered on 18 February. Named *Rija*, she worked mainly between Germany and Scandinavia whilst on charter to Unifeeder, a Danish company which specialises in feeder services. She traded as *Rija* until 3 July 2007 when she was renamed *Victoria*. She worked in the Mediterranean during the summer and early autumn of 2007 but was back in northern Europe by the end of the year. We see her arriving from Southampton on 17 June 2009, the first day of new weekly service feedering CMA CGM containers between Le Havre, Avonmouth and Greenock. The service proved to be short-lived, the final sailing from Avonmouth being on 22 October.

This was not the first time that CMA CGM had feedered containers to and from Avonmouth. In late 2004 and 2005, the *Iduna* (ATG, 3585gt/91) called on a weekly service linking Le Havre to Zeebrugge, Cork and Avonmouth. This feeder ship was built at the Cassens shipyard in Emden where she was launched on 15 November 1991 with delivery being effected the following month. She has a 361TEU container capacity. *Lloyd's Register* notes that she was renamed *CMB Iduna* between 1994 and 1995 but there is no evidence of this in *Lloyd's Voyage Record*. Her first name change in fact seems to have taken place at Rotterdam on 25 May 2005 when she became *Sun Vita*, remaining on the same feeder route until the autumn of that year. In early October 2006, she was renamed *Spirit of Foynes* for a feeder service from Rotterdam to Foynes. In early March 2008 she reverted to *Sun Vita* and commenced trade in the Mediterranean.

The next four vessels were involved in the refrigerated trades. With eight 5-tonne derricks serving four hatches and four holds, the **Pacific Primorye** (MLT, 5131gt/86) has the classic outline of a refrigerated cargo ship built in Japan in the 1980s. She was constructed at the Hachinohe yard of Kitanihon Zosen K K and traded as **Ocean Rex** for the first ten years of her life. *Lloyd's Register* notes that she was renamed **Autumn Reefer** in 1996 but this seems to be incorrect. In fact,

she became **Sapphire Reefer** on 18 January 1996 and then **Green Tundra** at Zeebrugge on 18 June 1996. She was renamed **Pacific Primorye** at Gibraltar on 20 February 2006 and we see her passing Battery Point on 5 May in that year with a cargo of fresh produce from Alexandria. She reverted to her previous name of **Green Tundra** on 9 March 2007.

Although the number of refrigerated ships calling at Avonmouth has declined in recent years, there has nevertheless been some variety in the vessels seen. The **Rapa** (VCT, 10366gt/90), outward bound to Cristobal on 13 April 2008 after delivering fruit from Valparaiso, was built at the Brodogradiliste shipyard in Split. Originally named **Pacifik Frigo**, she had Croatian owners but was operated by Cool Carriers, a company established to operate refrigerated ships on behalf of owners. She left the Cool Carriers pool after being sold and renamed **Rapa** at Rotterdam in early June 2003. In autumn 2008, she was bought by Cypriot owners and renamed **Pacific Rime**. She suffered serious engine problems when leaving Bar, Montenegro, under her new name on 3 November 2008 and extensive repairs were required which lasted over three months.

The **Valparaiso Star** (BHS, 8945gt/89), outward bound to Argentina on 22 June 2008 after loading 36 empty containers, was built by Astlleros Espanoles at Seville. She was launched on 27 December 1988 and delivered in October 1989. Named **Del Monte Harvester**, she traded initially from Guayaquil in Ecuador and Puerto Limon in Costa Rica to Savannah and so was a frequent sight in the Panama Canal but by the late 1990s she was trading from Santo Tomas de Castilla in Guatemala to ports in the southern USA such as Galveston and Tampa with occasional seasonal transatlantic crossings to Dover and Antwerp. She became simply **Harvester** in 1999 and she was renamed **Valparaiso Star** at Los Angeles on 6 May 2004. Her 2-stroke 6-cylinder B&W engine of 13250bhp gives her a service speed of 20 knots.

The **Hansa Magdeburg** (DEU, 18334gt/03) passes Battery Point on 19 April 2009 at the end of a voyage from Chile with chilled produce. She was on voyage charter to Chilean owner CSAV and sailed on to Sheerness, Rotterdam and Hamburg after discharging a part cargo at Avonmouth. She was built in China by the Guangzhou Wenchong Shipyard Co Ltd and was launched as **Hansa Magdeburg** but entered service in April 2003 as **Cap Aguilar**. In 2005 she was chartered by A P Møller and renamed **Maersk Voshod** between late August 2005 and 1 October 2008 when she reverted to her original name. She has a container capacity of 1740TEU including 300 refrigerated containers. Like all refrigerated vessels, she requires good service speed and her 2-stroke 7-cylinder B&W engine of 21490bhp gives her 19.5 knots.

The ever-growing market for air travel ensures that a steady flow of tankers bring aviation fuel to Royal Portbury Dock and we look at four of them. Arriving with a cargo from Bantry Bay on 25 January 2007 is the BP tanker **British Excellence** (IOM, 23240gt/03). Built by the Hyundai Mipo Dockyard Co Ltd at Ulsan in South Korea, she was delivered as **Baltic Challenger** in October 2003. She was always operated by BP Amoco but did not gain her more suitable "British" name until early October 2005. Her registered owner was Maiden Over Ltd, a name that is probably more appealing to those in Britain and former Commonwealth countries than in Europe. She was bought by Greek owners and renamed **Hiona** in early April 2008. She is powered by a 2-stroke 7-cylinder MAN B&W engine of 12889bhp.

In 2003, World-Wide Shipping acquired Norwegian tanker operator Bergesen Shipping and the resultant company was called Bergesen Worldwide, the title being changed to BW Maritime in 2005. At the time of writing (mid 2010), the company operates fifty ships of which twelve are product tankers. One of the latter is the **BW Hudson** (PAN, 43737gt/07), built at Dalian in China, the full title of her builders being Dalian Shipbuilding Industry (Group) Co Ltd. She was completed in June 2007 and is powered by a 2-stroke 6-cylinder MAN-B&W engine of 16680bhp. She was arriving from Singapore with a part cargo of 20,000 tonnes of aviation fuel when photographed on 26 September 2008. The distinctive light green hull colour was always a feature of ships in the Bergesen fleet.

The brown upperworks of tankers operated by A/S Dampskibsselskabet TORM are frequent arrivals with jet fuel. The **Torm Cecilie** (DIS, 28381gt/01) is a good example. She was the third of four sisterships built for the company at the Jinhae shipyard of the Daedong Shipbuilding Co Ltd. Named **High Rod Falk** until 2003, this was modified to **Rod Falk** and she took her present name in 2005. She has a 2-stroke 6-cylinder B&W engine of 11107bhp. She is arriving on 14 April 2008 with 38,900 tonnes of fuel from Mina Abdullah in Kuwait.

The **Seamarlin** (DEU, 26548gt/07), inward bound on 3 December 2007 with a cargo of military aviation fuel from Loch Ewe in north-west Scotland, was built at the Lindenau shipyard located on the Kieler Förde north-west of the city of Kiel. She was handed over in July 2007 and was the last in a series of four sisterships built at the yard for German Tanker Shipping, a company established in 1998 but having its roots in the tanker fleet of Carl Büttner. Büttner traditionally named its tankers after fish in German and an image of the relevant fish was always placed prominently on the front of the ship's bridge. The new company has named its ships with the prefix "Sea" and has used the English name of the fish. Power comes from a 4-stroke 8-cylinder MAN-B&W engine of 15228bhp.

Imports of molasses arrive from various parts of the world and are often brought by interesting tankers. Some of these are notable because of their age, molasses being a relatively popular cargo for older vessels; others are notable because of their rarity. On 2 November 2007, the **Sichem Singapore** (ITA, 8562gt/06) was almost at the end of a voyage from Egypt to Avonmouth with 8,000 tonnes of molasses. She was built at the 21st Century Shipbuilding Co Ltd in Tongyeong and was handed over on 14 March 2006. She has twelve cargo tanks and is driven by a 2-stroke 6-cylinder MAN-B&W engine of 6037bhp. Her arrival was noteworthy because she rarely leaves the Mediterranean.

Most of the small cargoes of refined petroleum products are delivered to Avonmouth from Milford Haven but there are exceptions. The **Sten Tor** (NIS, 8594gt/99) was bringing her cargo of almost 11,000 tonnes of diesel fuel from Amsterdam when she passed Battery Point on a sunny but cold 30 January 2008. Built at the Jiangnan shipyard in Shanghai, she is driven by a 2-stroke 6-cylinder MAN-B&W engine with an output of 8362bhp. Like the **Sichem Singapore**, she has twelve cargo tanks. After ten years in Norwegian ownership, she was sold to Greek buyers in March 2009 and was renamed **Liquid Silver** under the Liberian flag.

The **Rudderman** (LBR, 4842gt/94) was the third of four similar tankers ordered by Rowbotham Tankships Ltd from the Malaysia Shipbuilding & Engineering yard at Johore. Completion of all four vessels was delayed and by the time that they were delivered, ownership was in the hands of a German investment consortium and the ships were bareboat chartered to P&O Tankships which had a 50% stake in the Rowbotham company. The charter was transferred to James Fisher & Sons plc on 31 December 1996. The **Rudderman** was launched on 22 April 1993 and was delivered in January 1994. Initial problems with manoeuvrability were solved with the fitting of Schilling twin rudders and all four tankers proved to be popular with crews. She has been a regular caller at Avonmouth bringing refined products from Milford Haven and we see her near the end of such a voyage on 27 January 2008. Because of a downturn in business, she was handed back to her owners at Portland on 23 July 2009. She was sold late in 2009 and renamed **Yema**.

The **Arduity** (GBR, 1926gt/81) was one of four similar tankers built by the Goole Shipbuilding & Repairing Co Ltd. Three were constructed for F T Everard but this tanker was ordered by Shell UK Oil. Launched on 5 June 1981, she was delivered to Shell as **Shell Seafarer** in November 1981. In June 1993, Shell happily reverted to the tradition of naming their tankers after shells and the **Shell Seafarer** was renamed **Asprella** in a ceremony at Ellesmere Port. In the late 1990s, Shell decided to dispose of its coastal fleet and the **Asprella** joined her three sisterships in the Everard fleet, being renamed **Arduity** in mid-September 1999. After just over seven years she was sold to owners in Malta. She left Cork on 7 January 2007, called at Gibraltar on 13 January and arrived at Malta four days later. She was renamed **Salina Bay** on 8 February and entered service as a bunkering tanker. We see her passing the Point on 28 July 2006 with a cargo of diesel and unleaded motor spirit.

The Palmali company was established in Istanbul in 1998. Initially it was merely an agency offering services to ships passing through the Dardanelles and the Bosphorus. The company soon ventured into the ownership of ships, especially those able to navigate on Russia's inland waterways, and it sought to become a major operator in the Black Sea and Caspian Sea. Its growth has been phenomenal and its vessels now trade worldwide. The **Agdash** (MLT, 7833gt/07) is the eighth tanker in a series begun in 2004 and all built at the Krasnoye Sormovo shipyard in Nizhniy Novgorod, a city formerly known as Gorky. These are the biggest sea-river ships built at the yard and also are the biggest ships able to sail in the Caspian Sea. The first six in the series were built for owners in Azerbaijan. Palmali ordered the next three and has since ordered two more. The **Agdash**, the second built for Palmali, was launched on 9 September 2007 and handed over on 23 October. She is seen passing Battery Point late in the afternoon of 23 February 2009 with refined petroleum products from Fawley.

The **Yuzhnyy** (UKR, 1896gt/84) delivered a cargo of 3,000 tonnes of molasses from Moerdijk to Royal Portbury Dock on 10 November 2001. She is one of a large number of identical tankers built during the 1980s at the Ivan Dimitrov shipyard in Rousse, Bulgaria. These were intended to be bunkering tankers in Russian ports and this example was built for Sevastopol and was named **Manganary** until 1997 when she took her current name. In 2003, she was converted to a vegetable oil tanker and has traded throughout northern and southern Europe although her registered owners continue to be Sevastopol Sea Fishing Port. Her engine is a 4-stroke 8-cylinder SKL diesel of 1200bhp.

Two vessels have been recently detained in Avonmouth for a significant period. The **Ben Aicha** (MAR, 16477gt/87) was built at the Dunkerque yard of Chantiers du Nord et de la Mediterranée. She was launched on 12 April 1986 and delivered in March of the following year. She is powered by a 2-stroke 6-cylinder Sulzer engine of 11,500bhp. She has 24 cargo tanks and 9 pumps. She arrived at Avonmouth from the Indian port of Chennai (Madras) with a cargo of molasses on 22 April 2008 and was subsequently examined by port state control surveyors. They found 21 deficiencies, 2 of which were deemed sufficiently serious to detain the tanker in port until they were rectified. The serious deficiencies included a lack of training displayed by her crew during fire and abandon ship drills, whilst other deficiencies included a lifeboat rudder that had not been properly maintained and an incinerator which had been inoperative for over two months. After all deficiencies had been rectified, she was released on 20 May and we see her at the start of a voyage to Stavanger on the following day. In March 2010, she was sold to Tunisian flag operators and renamed **Zembra**.

The second vessel was the *Vivara* (MLT, 5659gt/00) which arrived at Avonmouth as *OMG Kolpino* with a cargo of fertiliser from Abu Kir on 17 March 2009. After arrival, her crew blocked unloading operations, claiming that they had not been paid since December 2008. She was placed under arrest and eventually sold to German owners. We see her leaving on her maiden voyage for her new owners on 27 July 2009. An angular and unattractive vessel, her hull was built at the Severnaya shipyard in St Petersburg and she was completed for Norwegian owners in April 2000 by Stocznia Marynarki Wojennej at Gdynia. Originally named *Moksheim*, she became *OMG Kolpino* in late April 2008.

We next look at two vessels which passed Battery Point near the end of their maiden commercial voyage. The first one is the tanker **Bro Alma** (NLD, 12162gt/08) which delivered a 9,000 tonne cargo of liquid urea ammonium nitrate fertiliser from Constanta on 23 August 2008. She was built at the Celik Tekne shipyard in Tuzla, near Istanbul, and delivered in July 2008. Modern day ship ownership is an astonishingly complex business in all senses of the word. The first three letters of her name are taken from Broström, a Swedish shipowning company.

During the last two decades, the company has been involved in a series of takeovers and mergers. In 2009, it became part of the huge Danish A P Møller - Maersk group which also includes the Svitzer tug fleet. The **Bro Alma** is commercially managed by Broström but technical management is the responsibility of a Dutch company, Marin Ship Management. To complicate still further, she was one of six tankers ordered by Broström and built in partnership with Dünya Shipping, of Istanbul, the partners having three vessels each.

Our second vessel noted at the end of her maiden commercial voyage is the **_Bottiglieri Challenger_** (ITA, 51255gt/10) which arrived on 3 April 2010 with a cargo of coal from Richards Bay in South Africa. She was launched at the New Jiangsu Yangzijiang shipyard in Jianjiang, China, on 14 November 2009 and is the fourth of ten sister vessels ordered from the yard by Italian owner Giuseppe Bottiglieri who has been urging owners to renew their fleets during the current period of economic recession. In 2007, Bottiglieri determined to have a modern dry cargo fleet ready for the completion of the widening and deepening of the Panama Canal which should be completed by 2014. The bulk carrier is understood to have been time chartered by Glencore International AG, one of the wealthiest (and most controversial) companies in the world which produces and sources raw materials for industrial consumers.

The two most successful operators of dry cargo ships in the UK are both based on the Isle of Wight. The oldest and biggest of these companies is Carisbrooke Shipping whose fleet now includes much larger vessels than the coasters with which it was originally associated. The **Anja C** (GBR, 5604gt/06), seen arriving with a cargo of grain from Canada on 3 November 2007, was built by the Jiangsu Yangzjiang Shipbuilding Co Ltd at Jiangyin in China and delivered to her owners in July 2006. She is powered by a 2-stroke 7-cylinder MAN-B&W engine of 3807bhp.

The second fleet based on the Isle of Wight is Faversham Ships Ltd, a company which retained its name after moving to the island from Kent. The fleet has been built upon high quality second-hand vessels, the **Vedette** (IOM, 2033gt/90) being a good example. This ship was built at the Bodewes shipyard in Hoogezand for Beck's. This yard is on a canal east of Groningen in the north of the Netherlands and in the mid-20th century there were over 50 shipyards in the area. Closures and mergers have resulted in the survival of only a handful. The **Vedette** was launched on 27 October 1990 and handed over to Beck's during December. She is powered by a 4-stroke 6-cylinder MaK engine of 1795bhp. Seen on 4 September 2007, she was bringing 2750 tonnes of fertiliser from Amsterdam. On 27 April 2010, she was sold to Turkish owners and was renamed **Alara** under the flag of St Kitts & Nevis. Just visible ahead of the port bow of the **Vedette** is the **Isambard Brunel**, the Port of Bristol's survey vessel.

Inward bound from Glasgow on 26 November 2009 to load 5700 tonnes of grain for Belfast is the **Apollo Eagle** (ATG, 4255gt/72), one of four similar vessels built by A Vuijk & Zonen's shipyard at Capelle a/d IJssel. She was launched on 24 August 1971 and delivered in April 1972. Initially named **Christiane Schulte**, she became **Christa** in 1987 but reverted to her original name in Autumn 1992. She became **Apollo Eagle** in 1998. In early January 1992, she went to the yard of Estaleiros Navais de Viana do Castelo in Portugal where she was fitted with an additional cargo section, increasing her length by 4,8 metres and also increasing her tonnages from 3892gt and 6209dwt to 4255gt and 6341dwt. She resumed trade on 14 February 1992.

The search for cheap new vessels has taken northern European owners to a wide variety of locations. The **Dinteldijk** (NLD, 2984gt/07) was the second in a series of 4450 deadweight dry cargo ships built in Goa by the Chowgule & Co Pvt Ltd. She was launched on 17 June 2007 and delivered to her Dutch owners on 20 December. For her delivery voyage to northern Europe, she was lucky enough to have a cargo of granite taken from the Indian port of Chennai to Fredrikstad in Norway. In this photograph we see her arriving with a cargo of animal feed from Bordeaux on 27 November 2009.

We now see two ships built in the Netherlands. The **Portgarth** is about to take a stern line from the **Vlieland** (NLD, 3990gt/05) as she passes the Point on 10 February 2010. She was built at the Ferus Smit shipyard in Westerbroek, a small town on the Winschoterdiep canal in the north of the Netherlands. She is powered by a 4-stroke 8-cylinder MaK engine of 3589bhp and is owned by Kustvaart Harlingen, a consortium of four young Dutch captains who have invested heavily in modern tonnage and have earned a fine reputation as they renew and build up their fleet. On this voyage, she was carrying 5044 tonnes of sunflower seeds from Kherson in the Ukraine.

The arrival of the *Barizo* (ESP, 2999gt/99) to load a cargo of grain for Pasajes on 21 September 2008 could have passed unnoticed but it ought not to have done so for at least two reasons. Firstly, we do not see too many ships flying the Spanish flag. The second reason is that her maiden voyage brought her to Avonmouth, arriving from Amsterdam on 3 September 1999. Her hull was built in Romania by Santierul Naval Damen Galati and launched on 30 March 1999. This was then towed to the Netherlands and arrived at Delfzijl on 4 May. Three days later, the hull arrived at the Damen shipyard in Hoogezand for fitting out and the completed vessel was towed to Emden for drydocking on 19 August. One week later she arrived in Amsterdam and on 27 August was officially delivered to the Enzian Shipping Company of Berne, Switzerland, and was christened *Kathrin* by Mrs Kathrin Müller. She was one of four Damen Combi Freighter 5050 ships in the Enzian fleet. On the evening of 12 February 2006, she ran aground briefly on the Goodwin Sands after her Master had fallen asleep. The *Kathrin* was bought by Spanish owners on 21 March 2007 and was renamed *Barizo*. It should be evident by now that the author does not belong to that school of photographers who claim that the perfect ship photograph has no foreground or background interest.

The *Kizhi* (RUS, 2829gt/86) represents an interesting stage in the development of Russian sea/river ships. She was built by Santierul Naval Oltenita in Romania and was originally named *Volgo-Don 5093*, one of the large Volgo-Don class built for navigation on Russia's inland waterways. When the Soviet Union collapsed in 1991, its state-owned merchant fleet was hived off to private ownership. Many readers will remember the acute shortage of currency in Russia following the collapse of the Soviet system and the new shipowners were desperate to earn currency elsewhere. Two Volgo-Don vessels were given permission to trade in the Gulf of Finland in 1992. Experience with these vessels suggested they were not suitable for seagoing work in their existing configuration so several were shortened in the mid-1990s to make them better sea ships. This example went to the Cassens shipyard in Emden to be shortened by some 33 metres. We see her on 16 April 2008 as she arrives in ballast from Waterford; she loaded 2,500 tonnes of scrap for Bilbao. Outward bound is the vehicle carrier *Figaro* (SGP, 50681gt/81).

The new classes of Russian sea/river ships have been designed with sea trade in mind. They are able to carry only part cargoes when trading on the Russian inland waterway system. A good example is the **Professor Katsman** (MLT, 4970gt/08) built at the Oka shipyard in Navashino. She can carry 4925 tonnes of cargo at sea on a draught of 4,2 metres but only 3720 tonnes in rivers on a draught of 3,6 metres. Nevertheless, this would be a good cargo on such a relatively shallow draught. Delivered in December 2008, she is the twelfth vessel in the Rusich class and was to have been named **Rusich-12** in series with the previous eleven vessels. The identity of the person who gave his name to the ship is uncertain, although it is known that there was a professor of drama of that name at what was the University of Leningrad. Outward bound to St Petersburg on 30 July 2009, she had discharged animal feed from Liepaja.

The import of gypsum, mainly from Garrucha in Spain, continues to be a significant trade for Royal Portbury Dock. Most cargoes are brought by the **Yeoman Bank** which featured in *Passing the Point* and which, incidentally, now has a black hull rather than the red one depicted in that book. When she is unavailable because of drydocking or trade requirements elsewhere, it is necessary to use other ships and on a rather overcast 23 November 2008 the **Telnes** (MLT, 6944gt/82) was noted inward bound with 9640 tonnes of gypsum. She was launched at the Ulsteinvik shipyard of Kleven Mek Verksted on 17 October 1981 and delivered to her owners on 27 February 1982. She is powered by a 4-stroke 6-cylinder Werkspoor engine of 4600bhp.

For no apparent reason, blue has become the standard hull colour for many coastal vessels over the last thirty years. Grey perhaps would come second in a popularity list, but to combine a grey hull with grey superstructure is not aesthetically pleasing as evidenced by this view of the **Simon B** (ATG, 2590gt/85) approaching Battery Point on 8 August 2008 after delivering a cargo of stone from Belfast. She was the first of only four coasters of the Type 130b design from the J J Sietas shipyard and traded as **Paula** until 2006 when bought by Guido Buck and renamed **Simon B**. Within a few weeks of this photograph, she was sold to Dutch owners, renamed **Maple** - and repainted blue.

The growth of wind farms is evident throughout the UK but there are critics who draw attention to the visual impact of the turbines and also to the energy used in manufacturing and transporting them. In 2007, the Bristol Port Company built three turbines which deliver 75% of the electricity required by the port. The *Cimbris* (GIB, 3173gt/03) brought the tower sections from Emden in Germany and is seen passing Battery Point on 8 July 2007. Built at the Rousse shipyard in Bulgaria, she was launched as *Osteriff* but delivered as *Cimbris* in June 2003.

The hull of the **Sandra** (ANT, 2545gt/00) was built by Daewoo-Mangalia Heavy Industries in Romania and the ship was towed to the Damen shipyard in Bergum for completion. Driven by a 4-stroke 8-cylinder MaK engine of 2066bhp, she is an example of the Damen Combi Freighter 3850 design which has become hugely popular with owners and charterers. Although officially delivered on 29 December 2000, she did not complete trials until 2 February 2001. We see her arriving from Antwerp on 19 April 2009 with a cargo of wind turbine blades destined for a small windfarm in South Wales. She left Avonmouth on 21 April and should have sailed the short distance to Royal Portbury Dock but a communication breakdown resulted in her sailing to Barry Roads where she turned back and berthed at Royal Portbury to load grain for the Spanish port of Marin.

Readers will be well aware of the continuing cuts in defence expenditure which have resulted in a depleted Royal Navy fleet. Operational warships have little time for courtesy visits so we now rarely see them in the upper reaches of the Bristol Channel. On 20 February 2009, however, **HMS Cornwall** did arrive for a brief stay in Avonmouth. She was the first Batch 3 Type 22 frigate, a design based on the Broadsword class but some seventeen metres longer. She was built by Yarrow Shipbuilders on the River Clyde and was launched by Diana Princess of Wales on 14 October 1985. Later in 2009 she was deployed on counter piracy operations in the Gulf of Aden as part of NATO's Operation Ocean Shield.

The **Zeus**, photographed on 26 May 2009, is the only active cable repair ship in the US Navy and she has the further distinction of being the first vessel of her kind to be designed and built by the US Navy. She fulfils three major roles, one of which is to carry out maintenance work on the Sound Surveillance System (SOSUS) which is a network of strategically placed sonar sensors that provide early warning of submarines. The other two roles are oceanographic survey and the laying and maintenance of submarine cables. She can lay up to 1000 miles of cable in depths up to 9000 feet without resupply. Delivered to the Military Sealift Command in 1984, she was built by the National Steel & Shipbuilding Co, San Diego, California, and is diesel electric powered with five General Motors engines supplying power to two shafts. Shaft horsepower is 10,200.

We now look at a commercial cable ship. The cable ship **Dependable** (MHL, 12184gt/02), recently renamed from **Tyco Dependable**, was the fourth of six virtually identical vessels built for Tyco Telecommunications. Known as the Reliance class after the first ship in the series, these are modern ships fitted out for both undersea cable maintenance and the installation of new cables. She was built by the Keppel Hitachi shipyard in Singapore and was handed over to her owners on 19 November 2002. Tyco's fleet operations centre is in Baltimore, Maryland, but its UK depot in Avonmouth brings a variety of vessels to the port on cable-related work. In mid-March 2010, the owning company changed its name to Tyco Electronics Subsea Communications (TE SubCom) and the ships almost immediately lost their Tyco prefix. The **Dependable** was photographed on the evening of 12 April 2010.

Portishead Dock, like so many other former commercial ports, has now become a marina and is the home of a wide variety of small vessels including two lifeboats. The **Douglas Currie** was built in 1973 by Groves & Cutteridge, of Cowes. She was the last Solent class lifeboat to be built. She was intended to be mainly a relief vessel and was based in Scotland for much of her career in service with the Royal National Lifeboat Institution (RNLI). She was based at Kirkwall (1974 - 1975), Macduff (1975 - 1984), Fraserburgh (1985), Portpatrick (1986 - 1989) and then moved to Workington in Cumbria (1989 - 1992). Sold out of RNLI service in 1992, she was bought by Lions International and is understood to have served as the Los Cristianos lifeboat in the Canary Islands before being bought by the manager of Portishead marina. She was photographed on 18 December 2003.

The 1982-built **Mabel Alice** has a very different history and was born out of tragedy. She replaced the Penlee lifeboat **Solomon Browne** which was lost along with her crew when trying to rescue the crew of the stricken coaster **Union Star** in 1981. She was the 24th lifeboat in the Arun class and was the gift of Sir David Robinson who donated funds for four lifeboats. She was named after his wife. When in service at Newlyn, she was involved in various incidents. One of the first was the sad duty of having to return to shore the bodies of some of those who died when a British Airways Sikorksky S-61 helicopter crashed into the sea during a flight from Penzance to the Scilly Isles on 16 July 1983. Another notable incident occurred on 7 December 1994 when she assisted with the rescue of five people from the fishing vessel **Julian Paul** which had fouled her propeller when west of the Longships. Taken out of service and replaced by a new Severn class lifeboat in 2003, she was bought by Strathclyde police. In late 2008, she was bought by private owners in Berkeley and is seen here on 27 June 2009.

We now turn to workboats and begin with two dredgers. The **Sand Serin** (GBR, 1283gt/74) was built at the Clelands shipyard in Wallsend, having been subcontracted from the Port Glasgow yard of Ferguson Bros. She was launched on 19 September 1974 and delivered in December. She was an occasional visitor to the Bristol Channel, being called upon at particularly busy times or when other vessels were in drydock. Usually she worked in the Solent. We see her in the Bristol Channel on 15 September 2007. She did little work in 2008 and was laid up on the River Tees from late December. On 28 July 2009, she was towed from the Tees to Waterford and although offered for resale, it was assumed that she would eventually be scrapped.

There is a constant requirement to ensure that the main shipping channel on the approach to the port is maintained at a suitable depth to allow the passage of the largest ships able to enter the port. The dredging work is contracted out to UK Dredging, a subsidiary of Associated British Ports (ABP), and this company's **UKD Dolphin** (GBR, 1742gt/84) is often seen working in the channel. She was built for Dutch owners by IHC Sliedrecht, a Dutch builder specialising in the construction of dredgers, and was originally named **Dolphin**. Launched on 19 April 1984, she was delivered during June. She was acquired by ABP in 1988 and was renamed **Humber Dolphin**, her new name indicating her intended area of work. Moving to South Wales in 1994, she was appropriately renamed **Welsh Dolphin** and became **UKD Dolphin** in 1997 when UK Dredging was established as a wholly-owned subsidiary company of ABP.

Our focus turns now to tugs. The **Portgarth** (GBR, 262gt/95) featured in *Passing the Point* but in her original Cory colours. When photographed on 11 February 2008, she was wearing the latest version of Svitzer livery. Her funnel bears the image of a four-bladed propeller which had replaced the traditional Svitzer logo of a Maltese Cross. Surprisingly the new logo was applied only to tug funnels; it did not become the company's general logo. Completed at the Damen shipyard in Gorinchem on a hull built at Severodvinsk in Russia, she is an example of the Damen ASD3110 standard design. Her two 4-stroke 9-cylinder Kromhout engines each of 2026bhp give her a bollard pull of 50 tonnes. As these notes are being written in mid-2010, there are rumours that she will soon be moved away from the Bristol Channel.

The sister tugs **Svitzer Bristol** and **Svitzer Brunel** (both GBR, 366gt/03) are seen awaiting the arrival of a vessel on 30 January 2008. Both tugs were built in Spain by Astilleros Zamakona at Viscaya near Bilbao. They are powered by two 4-stroke 6-cylinder Niigata engines each of 2200bhp which provide a bollard pull of 60 tonnes.

Again the tugs carry the 4-blade propeller logo on their funnel rather than the Maltese Cross which adorned the **Svitzer Bristol** on page 69 of *Passing the Point*. Readers may wish to look closely at the above photograph to spot a feature which distinguishes one tug from the other.

When the **Bargarth** (GBR, 210gt/79) was photographed on 14 April 2008, she was making one of her rare visits to the English side of the Bristol Channel. She was the last of four tugs ordered from Scott & Sons Ltd at Bowling on the River Clyde. Allocated to Forth Tugs Ltd, a subsidiary of Cory Ship Towage, her owners required firefighting capability because of the predominance of tanker vessels at Grangemouth and this meant changes to the original design for her and a sister vessel. She is driven by two 4-stroke 6-cylinder Ruston engines each of 1100bhp which drive two Voith-Schneider propellers and give a bollard pull of 24 tonnes. She was launched as **Laggan** on 25 June 1979 and delivered to Forth Tugs on 12 November. She was renamed **Forth** in 1987 and became **Bargarth** in 2003 with Svitzer Marine now as owners after being transferred to the South Wales fleet. She was sold to Irish operators Fastnet Shipping in autumn 2009 and left Cardiff bound for Waterford on 9 November 2009.

There are many advantages in having a large tug fleet based in various ports, one of these being that tugs can be moved around to meet varying operational requirements. A disadvantage is that tugs with names that are associated with a specific area can be moved to an area where that name has little relevance. This happened when the **Svitzer Bevois** (GBR, 250gt/85) moved from Southampton to the Bristol Channel in April 2008. She was originally named **Sir Bevois** after the legendary founder of Southampton and was the second of a pair of tugs built for Red Funnel by McTay Marine at Bromborough on the River Mersey. She was launched on 2 June 1985 and delivered in August of that year. Her renaming from **Sir Bevois** (pronounced "Beevis") to **Svitzer Bevois** in 2007 may suit her owner's company image but has resulted in a meaningless name. She has two 4-stroke 6-cylinder Kromhout engines each of 1360bhp which give her a bollard pull of 35 tonnes. We see her on the starboard quarter of the K-line operated bulk carrier **Mitose** (PAN, 40028gt/08) which was arriving with a cargo of coal from Riga on 16 June 2009.

After a competitive tendering process in 1994, the newly-established West Coast Towing Co Ltd won the contract to provide towage services for the British Steel Corporation vessels at Port Talbot tidal harbour and for those calling at Swansea to handle British Steel cargoes. The company soon began to offer towage at other ports in South Wales and a small fleet of second-hand tugs was built up including several of Russian origin. The *E. L. Preston* (GBR, 182gt/92) was a typical example, built as *Imakon* at the Gorokhovets shipyard in Russia and renamed after arrival in Wales. By 2000/01 West Coast Towing had lost many of the contracts it had won and it was bought by Wijsmuller BV and this tug was renamed *Butegarth* in 2002. This proved to be short-lived as in 2003 she was bought by Estonian owners and renamed *Vega I*, this being equally brief because she returned to Russian ownership the following year when renamed *Poseydon*. Power comes from two 4-stroke 8-cylinder Pervomaysk engines, each of 802bhp. West Coast Towing tugs did very little work on the English side of the Bristol Channel, this tug's attendance on the *Gem* (page 26) being a rare example.

The **Fighter** (BEL, 517gt/77) was built by Scheepswerf van Rupelmonde in Belgium. She was launched on 8 March 1977 and delivered during the following month. She was powered by a 4-stroke 16-cylinder Cockerill engine of 4079bhp and had a 55 tonne bollard pull. Her owners were Antwerp-based Unie van Redding en Sleepdienst (URS) and she was initially stationed at Vlissingen. She and a sister vessel were built at a time of rapid development of oil and gas fields in the North Sea and it was intended that she would undertake offshore towage in addition to harbour work. She was involved in many salvage duties but her most important role was during the tragic loss of the ferry **Herald of Free Enterprise** at Zeebrugge on 6 March 1987. Not only did her crew assist in the rescue of many survivors but the tug also had the sad duty of delivering many bodies to the shore.

The valiant work of the crew on that occasion was recognised by the Belgian royal family and by Margaret Thatcher, then British Prime Minister. They were most moved, though, by a note of thanks from 14-year-old Nicola Simpson who was rescued but whose mother died in the tragedy. That note remained pinned in the tug's wheelhouse. We see the **Fighter** on 13 September 2006 as she towed the barge **Smit Anambas** on which is a new crane for the bulk terminal in Royal Portbury Dock. She was taken out of service in 2007 and, having been stripped, was towed to Rotterdam where she would be used as a base for students of performing arts but with an exhibition established on board to keep alive her rich and important history.

The Wagenborg company is based in the Delfzijl area in the north of the Netherlands. For over a century its ships have been a familiar sight in ports throughout Europe and now much further afield. The company is also involved in warehousing and road transport. It has a small fleet of tugs based in Delfzijl and used mainly for harbour towage but also for contract towage much further afield. The hull of the **Watergeus** (NLD, 134gt/95) was built in Poland by Stocznia Tczew and completion was undertaken at the Damen shipyard in Gorinchem. Power comes from two 4-stroke 12-cylinder Wärtsilä engines, each of 904bhp, which drive two fixed pitch propellers. She has a bollard pull of 25.5 tonnes. She was photographed on 12 May 2008 with the barge **Skyline Barge 17** in tow. The purpose of the visit will be explained in the following caption.

The **Mersey Mammoth** (GBR, 1793gt/86) was built at the Ravenstein shipyard in Deest. Generally described as a floating crane, she is more accurately described as a crane pontoon. She was launched on 15 August 1986 and delivered to the Mersey Docks & Harbour Company in October of that year. As her name implies, she is based on the River Mersey but is often called away for contract work elsewhere. She had been hired by the Bristol Port Company to assist in the removal and lifting of the troublesome middle lock gates at Royal Portbury Dock. She arrived on 27 May 2008 and lifted the gates on to **Skyline Barge 17** for delivery to Rotterdam where they would be repaired.

The environmental benefits of water transport over road transport ought to be self-evident and politicians are increasingly keen to present their green credentials. Despite this, the transfer of freight from road to water has yet to gain momentum. One glimmer of hope was offered by the construction of the barge *Terra Marique* in 2004 for the transport of heavy lifts. She was ordered from Dutch shipbuilder Damen and her hull was built at that company's yard in the Ukraine but fitted out in the Netherlands. She is a multipurpose vessel able to handle a wide variety of cargoes loaded and discharged at remote locations. She has a specially strengthened hull to allow loading on beaches. She can also semi-submerge and thus load smaller vessels. She was photographed as she approached Avonmouth on 23 November 2008 with a 310 tonne transformer for Didcot power station.

Towing the *Terra Marique* on the above occasion was the tug *South* (ANT, 259gt/08). She is one of four tugs built at the Kian Juan Dockyard, Miri Sarawak, in Malaysia. It should take little imagination to work out the name of the other three tugs but in case help is needed, we can tell readers that her owners have a fifth tug named *Compass*. The *South* was launched as *Danga South 9* but was soon renamed following purchase by Avra Towage, a Dutch company with extensive interests in South-East Asia. Her two Cummins engines have a total power of 2432bhp and give her a bollard pull of 32 tonnes.

Although the Bristol Channel remains popular with day trippers, the number of vessels offering sailings is but a fraction of those in the days of the White Funnel fleet of P & A Campbell. The ***Oldenburg*** (GBR, 294gt/58) is an occasional visitor to the upper reaches of the Bristol Channel. She is usually to be found transporting passengers between Bideford and the island of Lundy. She was built at the Detlef Hegemann Rolandwerft shipyard in Bremen, being launched on 29 March 1958 and delivered on 6 August. Initially she was used for a ferry service between the German mainland and the Frisian island of Wangerooge. In 1975 she began to make duty-free shopping cruises around the Frisian islands. She was acquired by the Landmark Trust for service to Lundy Island in November 1985 and was refurbished at Appledore in 1986. In 1999 she was fitted with new engines, these being two 4-stroke 6-cylinder Cummins engines each of 431bhp which drive two fixed pitch propellers. She has a certificate for 359 passengers. We see her passing Battery Point on 5 July 1998.

Being claimed as the world's last seagoing paddle steamer, the **Waverley** is possibly better known than the **Balmoral** (GBR, 735gt/49) but the latter vessel has fulfilled an important role in offering day sailings in the Bristol Channel during the summer months since 1986. She spends some time in other areas of the UK during the early and late holiday season. She was built by John I Thornycroft & Co Ltd at Southampton and was launched on 27 June 1949. She was built for the Red Funnel ferry service between Southampton and Cowes and represented the company at the Coronation Fleet Review in 1953. Withdrawn by Red Funnel in 1968, she was chartered by P & A Campbell the following year. After eleven years,

she was taken out of service when the Campbell company ceased its passenger sailings. She languished at Dundee as a plan for her to become a floating restaurant proved abortive and was acquired by the Waverley Steam Navigation Company in 1985. After being refurbished on the Clyde in late 1985 and early 1986, she entered service in 1986. Upgrading has continued since then, her original 2-stroke Newbury Sirron engines being replaced by two 4-stroke 6-cylinder Grenå engines during March and April 2003. She was photographed heading up channel in May 2005.

We close the book with a general view looking down channel from Battery Point. The **Brunhilde Salamon** (MHL, 39126gt/01) is inward bound to Royal Portbury Dock with a 57190 tonnes of coal from Riga on 21 October 2007. The German-owned bulk carrier was built by Kanasashi Heavy Industries Co Ltd at Toyohashi in Japan. She was named **Lake Camellia** until late January 2005. Power comes from a 2-stroke 7-cylinder MAN-B&W engine of 15014bhp. The controversial Portland stone memorial to the left of the photograph is dedicated to the seafarers of the West Country who "since the Middle Ages, on voyages of discovery in times of peace and war, have passed this point, some never to return."